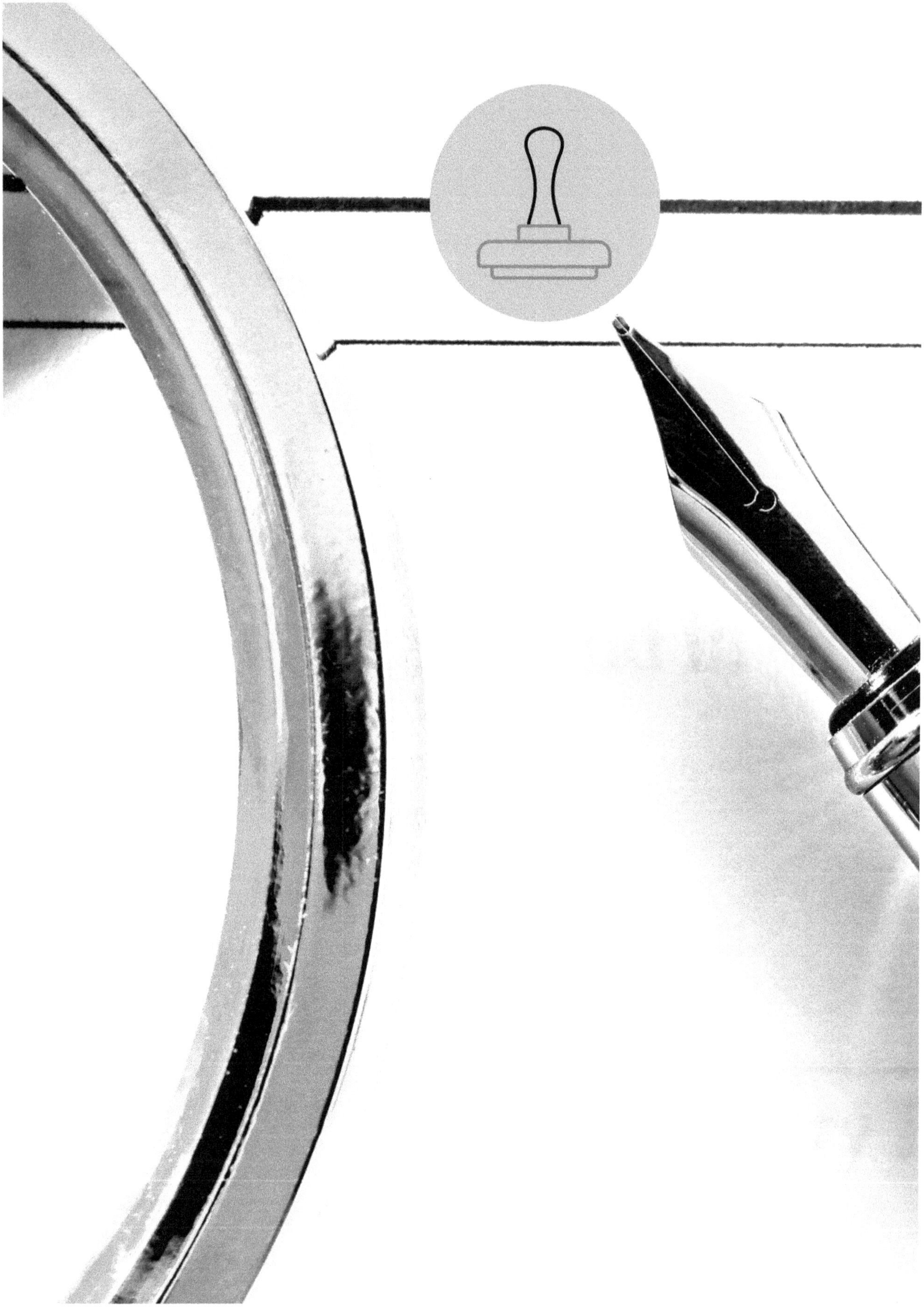

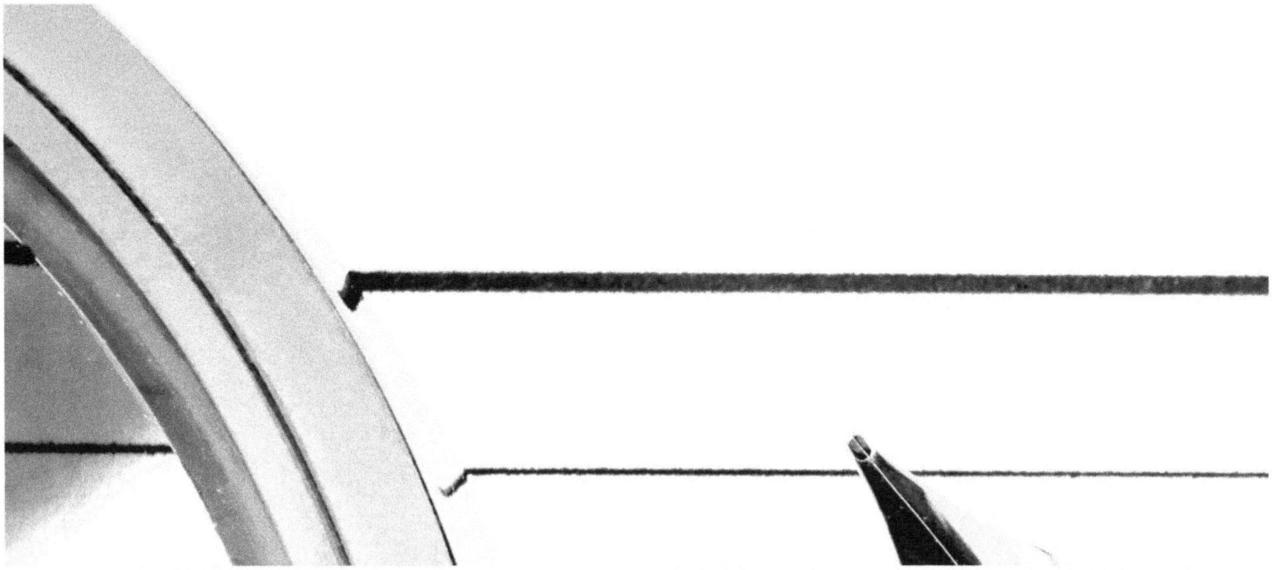

Notary Journal

This Book Belongs To:

Name

Present Address

Permanent Address

Business Address & Telephone

Mobile

E-mail

Fax

Website

Blood Group

In Case Of Emergency, Please Contact

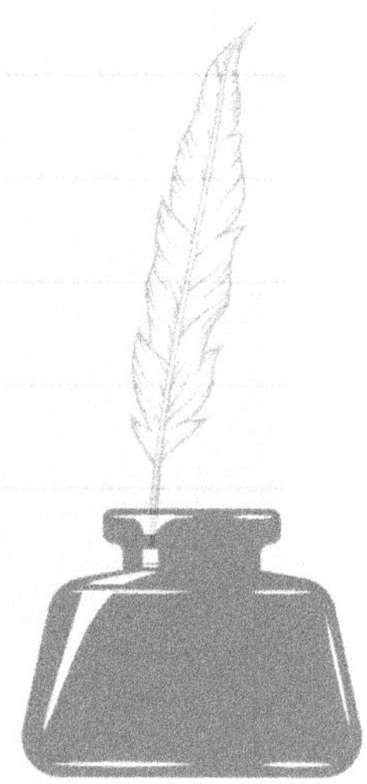

ENTRY # Month : M T W T F S S Page No.

Record Number : $Fee Thumb Print :

Notarized Type : Date Notarized :

Document Type : Document Date :

Service Performed

☐ Certification ☐ Acknowledgment ☐ Oath ☐ Jurat ☐

Identification

☐ Passport ☐ Known Personally ☐ ID Card ☐ Driver's License ☐

#ID Card

ID Number Issued Date : Expires :

Issued By :

☐ Individual ☐ Witness

Printed Name : Printed Name :

Address : Address :

Contact Info : Contact Info :

Signature : Signature :

Take Note

Notes

ENTRY # Month : M T W T F S S Page No.

Record Number : $Fee [ ] Thumb Print :

Notarized Type : Date Notarized :

Document Type : Document Date :

Service Performed

☐ Certification ☐ Acknowledgment ☐ Oath ☐ Jurat ☐

Identification

☐ Passport ☐ Known Personally ☐ ID Card ☐ Driver's License ☐

#ID Card

ID Number [ ] Issued Date : Expires :

Issued By :

☐ Individual ☐ Witness

Printed Name : Printed Name :

Address : Address :

Contact Info : Contact Info :

Signature : Signature :

Take Note

Notes

ENTRY # Month : M T W T F S S Page No.

Record Number : $Fee Thumb Print :

Notarized Type : Date Notarized :

Document Type : Document Date :

Service Performed

☐ Certification ☐ Acknowledgment ☐ Oath ☐ Jurat ☐

Identification

☐ Passport ☐ Known Personally ☐ ID Card ☐ Driver's License ☐

#ID Card

ID Number Issued Date : Expires :

Issued By :

☐ Individual ☐ Witness

Printed Name : Printed Name :

Address : Address :

Contact Info : Contact Info :

Signature : Signature :

Take Note

Notes

ENTRY # Month : M T W T F S S Page No.

Record Number : $Fee ☐ Thumb Print :

Notarized Type : Date Notarized :

Document Type : Document Date :

Service Performed

☐ Certification ☐ Acknowledgment ☐ Oath ☐ Jurat ☐

Identification

☐ Passport ☐ Known Personally ☐ ID Card ☐ Driver's License ☐

#ID Card

ID Number ☐ Issued Date : Expires :

Issued By :

☐ Individual ☐ Witness

Printed Name : Printed Name :

Address : Address :

Contact Info : Contact Info :

Signature : Signature :

Take Note

Notes

ENTRY # Month : M T W T F S S Page No.

Record Number : $Fee ☐ Thumb Print :

Notarized Type : Date Notarized :

Document Type : Document Date :

Service Performed

☐ Certification ☐ Acknowledgment ☐ Oath ☐ Jurat ☐

Identification

☐ Passport ☐ Known Personally ☐ ID Card ☐ Driver's License ☐

#ID Card

ID Number ☐ Issued Date : Expires :

Issued By :

☐ Individual ☐ Witness

Printed Name : Printed Name :

Address : Address :

Contact Info : Contact Info :

Signature : Signature :

Take Note

Notes

ENTRY # Month : M T W T F S S Page No.

Record Number : $Fee [ ] Thumb Print :

Notarized Type : Date Notarized :

Document Type : Document Date :

Service Performed

☐ Certification ☐ Acknowledgment ☐ Oath ☐ Jurat ☐

Identification

☐ Passport ☐ Known Personally ☐ ID Card ☐ Driver's License ☐

#ID Card

ID Number [ ] Issued Date : Expires :

Issued By :

☐ Individual ☐ Witness

Printed Name : Printed Name :

Address : Address :

Contact Info : Contact Info :

Signature : Signature :

Take Note

Notes

ENTRY # Month : M T W T F S S Page No.

Record Number : $Fee Thumb Print :

Notarized Type : Date Notarized :

Document Type : Document Date :

Service Performed

☐ Certification ☐ Acknowledgment ☐ Oath ☐ Jurat ☐

Identification

☐ Passport ☐ Known Personally ☐ ID Card ☐ Driver's License ☐

#ID Card

ID Number Issued Date : Expires :

Issued By :

☐ Individual ☐ Witness

Printed Name : Printed Name :

Address : Address :

Contact Info : Contact Info :

Signature : Signature :

Take Note

Notes

ENTRY # Month : M T W T F S S Page No.

Record Number : $Fee [ ] Thumb Print :

Notarized Type : Date Notarized :

Document Type : Document Date :

Service Performed

☐ Certification ☐ Acknowledgment ☐ Oath ☐ Jurat ☐

Identification

☐ Passport ☐ Known Personally ☐ ID Card ☐ Driver's License ☐

#ID Card

ID Number [ ] Issued Date : Expires :

Issued By :

☐ Individual	☐ Witness
Printed Name :	Printed Name :
Address :	Address :
Contact Info :	Contact Info :
Signature :	Signature :

Take Note

Notes

ENTRY # Month : M T W T F S S Page No.

Record Number : $Fee [ ] Thumb Print :

Notarized Type : Date Notarized :

Document Type : Document Date :

Service Performed

☐ Certification ☐ Acknowledgment ☐ Oath ☐ Jurat ☐

Identification

☐ Passport ☐ Known Personally ☐ ID Card ☐ Driver's License ☐

#ID Card

ID Number [ ] Issued Date : Expires :

Issued By :

☐ Individual ☐ Witness

Printed Name : Printed Name :

Address : Address :

Contact Info : Contact Info :

Signature : Signature :

Take Note

Notes

ENTRY # Month : M T W T F S S Page No.

Record Number : $Fee [ ] Thumb Print :

Notarized Type : Date Notarized :

Document Type : Document Date :

Service Performed

☐ Certification ☐ Acknowledgment ☐ Oath ☐ Jurat ☐

Identification

☐ Passport ☐ Known Personally ☐ ID Card ☐ Driver's License ☐

#ID Card

ID Number [ ] Issued Date : Expires :

Issued By :

☐ Individual ☐ Witness

Printed Name : Printed Name :

Address : Address :

Contact Info : Contact Info :

Signature : Signature :

Take Note

Notes

ENTRY # Month : M T W T F S S Page No.

Record Number : $Fee [ ] Thumb Print :

Notarized Type : Date Notarized :

Document Type : Document Date :

Service Performed

☐ Certification ☐ Acknowledgment ☐ Oath ☐ Jurat ☐

Identification

☐ Passport ☐ Known Personally ☐ ID Card ☐ Driver's License ☐

#ID Card

ID Number [ ] Issued Date : Expires :

Issued By :

☐ Individual ☐ Witness

Printed Name : Printed Name :

Address : Address :

Contact Info : Contact Info :

Signature : Signature :

Take Note

Notes

ENTRY # Month : M T W T F S S Page No.

Record Number : $Fee Thumb Print :

Notarized Type : Date Notarized :

Document Type : Document Date :

Service Performed

☐ Certification ☐ Acknowledgment ☐ Oath ☐ Jurat ☐

Identification

☐ Passport ☐ Known Personally ☐ ID Card ☐ Driver's License ☐

#ID Card

ID Number Issued Date : Expires :

Issued By :

☐ Individual ☐ Witness

Printed Name : Printed Name :

Address : Address :

Contact Info : Contact Info :

Signature : Signature :

Take Note

Notes

ENTRY # Month : M T W T F S S Page No.

Record Number : $Fee [ ] Thumb Print :

Notarized Type : Date Notarized :

Document Type : Document Date :

Service Performed

☐ Certification ☐ Acknowledgment ☐ Oath ☐ Jurat ☐

Identification

☐ Passport ☐ Known Personally ☐ ID Card ☐ Driver's License ☐

#ID Card

ID Number [ ] Issued Date : Expires :

Issued By :

☐ Individual ☐ Witness

Printed Name : Printed Name :

Address : Address :

Contact Info : Contact Info :

Signature : Signature :

Take Note

Notes

ENTRY # Month : M T W T F S S Page No.

Record Number : $Fee [ ] Thumb Print :

Notarized Type : Date Notarized :

Document Type : Document Date :

Service Performed

☐ Certification ☐ Acknowledgment ☐ Oath ☐ Jurat ☐

Identification

☐ Passport ☐ Known Personally ☐ ID Card ☐ Driver's License ☐

#ID Card

ID Number [ ] Issued Date : Expires :

Issued By :

☐ Individual ☐ Witness

Printed Name : Printed Name :

Address : Address :

Contact Info : Contact Info :

Signature : Signature :

Take Note

Notes

ENTRY # Month : M T W T F S S Page No.

Record Number : $Fee Thumb Print :

Notarized Type : Date Notarized :

Document Type : Document Date :

Service Performed

☐ Certification ☐ Acknowledgment ☐ Oath ☐ Jurat ☐

Identification

☐ Passport ☐ Known Personally ☐ ID Card ☐ Driver's License ☐

#ID Card

ID Number Issued Date : Expires :

Issued By :

☐ Individual ☐ Witness

Printed Name : Printed Name :

Address : Address :

Contact Info : Contact Info :

Signature : Signature :

Take Note

Notes

ENTRY # Month : M T W T F S S Page No.

Record Number : $Fee ☐ Thumb Print :

Notarized Type : Date Notarized :

Document Type : Document Date :

Service Performed

☐ Certification ☐ Acknowledgment ☐ Oath ☐ Jurat ☐

Identification

☐ Passport ☐ Known Personally ☐ ID Card ☐ Driver's License ☐

#ID Card

ID Number ☐ Issued Date : Expires :

Issued By :

☐ Individual ☐ Witness

Printed Name : Printed Name :

Address : Address :

Contact Info : Contact Info :

Signature : Signature :

Take Note

Notes

ENTRY # Month : M T W T F S S Page No.

Record Number : $Fee Thumb Print :

Notarized Type : Date Notarized :

Document Type : Document Date :

Service Performed

☐ Certification ☐ Acknowledgment ☐ Oath ☐ Jurat ☐

Identification

☐ Passport ☐ Known Personally ☐ ID Card ☐ Driver's License ☐

#ID Card

ID Number Issued Date : Expires :

Issued By :

☐ Individual ☐ Witness

Printed Name : Printed Name :

Address : Address :

Contact Info : Contact Info :

Signature : Signature :

Take Note

Notes

ENTRY # Month : M T W T F S S Page No.

Record Number : $Fee [ ] Thumb Print :

Notarized Type : Date Notarized :

Document Type : Document Date :

Service Performed

☐ Certification ☐ Acknowledgment ☐ Oath ☐ Jurat ☐

Identification

☐ Passport ☐ Known Personally ☐ ID Card ☐ Driver's License ☐

#ID Card

ID Number [ ] Issued Date : Expires :

Issued By :

☐ Individual	☐ Witness
Printed Name :	Printed Name :
Address :	Address :
Contact Info :	Contact Info :
Signature :	Signature :

Take Note

Notes

ENTRY # Month : M T W T F S S Page No.

Record Number : $Fee [ ] Thumb Print :

Notarized Type : Date Notarized :

Document Type : Document Date :

Service Performed

☐ Certification ☐ Acknowledgment ☐ Oath ☐ Jurat ☐

Identification

☐ Passport ☐ Known Personally ☐ ID Card ☐ Driver's License ☐

#ID Card

ID Number [ ] Issued Date : Expires :

Issued By :

☐ Individual	☐ Witness
Printed Name :	Printed Name :
Address :	Address :
Contact Info :	Contact Info :
Signature :	Signature :

Take Note

Notes

ENTRY # Month : M T W T F S S Page No.

Record Number : $Fee ☐ Thumb Print :

Notarized Type : Date Notarized :

Document Type : Document Date :

Service Performed

☐ Certification ☐ Acknowledgment ☐ Oath ☐ Jurat ☐

Identification

☐ Passport ☐ Known Personally ☐ ID Card ☐ Driver's License ☐

#ID Card

ID Number ☐ Issued Date : Expires :

Issued By :

☐ Individual ☐ Witness

Printed Name : Printed Name :

Address : Address :

Contact Info : Contact Info :

Signature : Signature :

Take Note

Notes

ENTRY # Month : M T W T F S S Page No.

Record Number : $Fee [ ] Thumb Print :

Notarized Type : Date Notarized :

Document Type : Document Date :

Service Performed

☐ Certification ☐ Acknowledgment ☐ Oath ☐ Jurat ☐

Identification

☐ Passport ☐ Known Personally ☐ ID Card ☐ Driver's License ☐

#ID Card

ID Number [ ] Issued Date : Expires :

Issued By :

☐ Individual ☐ Witness

Printed Name : Printed Name :

Address : Address :

Contact Info : Contact Info :

Signature : Signature :

Take Note

Notes

ENTRY # Month : M T W T F S S Page No.

Record Number : $Fee [ ] Thumb Print :

Notarized Type : Date Notarized :

Document Type : Document Date :

Service Performed

☐ Certification ☐ Acknowledgment ☐ Oath ☐ Jurat ☐

Identification

☐ Passport ☐ Known Personally ☐ ID Card ☐ Driver's License ☐

#ID Card

ID Number [ ] Issued Date : Expires :

Issued By :

☐ Individual	☐ Witness
Printed Name :	Printed Name :
Address :	Address :
Contact Info :	Contact Info :
Signature :	Signature :

Take Note

Notes

ENTRY # Month : M T W T F S S Page No.

Record Number : $Fee [ ] Thumb Print :

Notarized Type : Date Notarized :

Document Type : Document Date :

Service Performed

☐ Certification ☐ Acknowledgment ☐ Oath ☐ Jurat ☐

Identification

☐ Passport ☐ Known Personally ☐ ID Card ☐ Driver's License ☐

#ID Card

ID Number [ ] Issued Date : Expires :

Issued By :

☐ Individual ☐ Witness

Printed Name : Printed Name :

Address : Address :

Contact Info : Contact Info :

Signature : Signature :

Take Note

Notes

ENTRY # Month : M T W T F S S Page No.

Record Number : $Fee Thumb Print :

Notarized Type : Date Notarized :

Document Type : Document Date :

Service Performed

☐ Certification ☐ Acknowledgment ☐ Oath ☐ Jurat ☐

Identification

☐ Passport ☐ Known Personally ☐ ID Card ☐ Driver's License ☐

#ID Card

ID Number Issued Date : Expires :

Issued By :

☐ Individual ☐ Witness

Printed Name : Printed Name :

Address : Address :

Contact Info : Contact Info :

Signature : Signature :

Take Note

Notes

ENTRY # Month : M T W T F S S Page No.

Record Number : $Fee Thumb Print :

Notarized Type : Date Notarized :

Document Type : Document Date :

Service Performed

☐ Certification ☐ Acknowledgment ☐ Oath ☐ Jurat ☐

Identification

☐ Passport ☐ Known Personally ☐ ID Card ☐ Driver's License ☐

#ID Card

ID Number Issued Date : Expires :

Issued By :

☐ Individual ☐ Witness

Printed Name : Printed Name :

Address : Address :

Contact Info : Contact Info :

Signature : Signature :

Take Note

Notes

ENTRY # Month : M T W T F S S Page No.

Record Number : $Fee [ ] Thumb Print :

Notarized Type : Date Notarized :

Document Type : Document Date :

Service Performed

☐ Certification ☐ Acknowledgment ☐ Oath ☐ Jurat ☐

Identification

☐ Passport ☐ Known Personally ☐ ID Card ☐ Driver's License ☐

#ID Card

ID Number [ ] Issued Date : Expires :

Issued By :

☐ Individual ☐ Witness

Printed Name : Printed Name :

Address : Address :

Contact Info : Contact Info :

Signature : Signature :

Take Note

Notes

ENTRY #	Month :	M T W T F S S	Page No.

Record Number :	$Fee [ ]	Thumb Print :

Notarized Type :	Date Notarized :

Document Type :	Document Date :

Service Performed

☐ Certification ☐ Acknowledgment ☐ Oath ☐ Jurat ☐

Identification

☐ Passport ☐ Known Personally ☐ ID Card ☐ Driver's License ☐

#ID Card

ID Number [ ] Issued Date : Expires :

Issued By :

☐ Individual ☐ Witness

Printed Name :	Printed Name :

Address :	Address :

Contact Info :	Contact Info :

Signature :	Signature :

Take Note

Notes

ENTRY # Month : M T W T F S S Page No.

Record Number : $Fee [ ] Thumb Print :

Notarized Type : Date Notarized :

Document Type : Document Date :

Service Performed

☐ Certification ☐ Acknowledgment ☐ Oath ☐ Jurat ☐

Identification

☐ Passport ☐ Known Personally ☐ ID Card ☐ Driver's License ☐

#ID Card

ID Number [ ] Issued Date : Expires :

Issued By :

☐ Individual ☐ Witness

Printed Name : Printed Name :

Address : Address :

Contact Info : Contact Info :

Signature : Signature :

Take Note

Notes

ENTRY # Month : M T W T F S S Page No.

Record Number : $Fee [ ] Thumb Print :

Notarized Type : Date Notarized :

Document Type : Document Date :

Service Performed

☐ Certification ☐ Acknowledgment ☐ Oath ☐ Jurat ☐

Identification

☐ Passport ☐ Known Personally ☐ ID Card ☐ Driver's License ☐

#ID Card

ID Number [ ] Issued Date : Expires :

Issued By :

☐ Individual ☐ Witness

Printed Name : Printed Name :

Address : Address :

Contact Info : Contact Info :

Signature : Signature :

Take Note

Notes

ENTRY # Month : M T W T F S S Page No.

Record Number : $Fee Thumb Print :

Notarized Type : Date Notarized :

Document Type : Document Date :

Service Performed

☐ Certification ☐ Acknowledgment ☐ Oath ☐ Jurat ☐

Identification

☐ Passport ☐ Known Personally ☐ ID Card ☐ Driver's License ☐

#ID Card

ID Number Issued Date : Expires :

Issued By :

☐ Individual ☐ Witness

Printed Name : Printed Name :

Address : Address :

Contact Info : Contact Info :

Signature : Signature :

Take Note

Notes

ENTRY # Month : M T W T F S S Page No.

Record Number : $Fee Thumb Print :

Notarized Type : Date Notarized :

Document Type : Document Date :

Service Performed

☐ Certification ☐ Acknowledgment ☐ Oath ☐ Jurat ☐

Identification

☐ Passport ☐ Known Personally ☐ ID Card ☐ Driver's License ☐

#ID Card

ID Number Issued Date : Expires :

Issued By :

☐ Individual ☐ Witness

Printed Name : Printed Name :

Address : Address :

Contact Info : Contact Info :

Signature : Signature :

Take Note

Notes

ENTRY # Month : M T W T F S S Page No.

Record Number : $Fee [ ] Thumb Print :

Notarized Type : Date Notarized :

Document Type : Document Date :

Service Performed

☐ Certification ☐ Acknowledgment ☐ Oath ☐ Jurat ☐

Identification

☐ Passport ☐ Known Personally ☐ ID Card ☐ Driver's License ☐

#ID Card

ID Number [ ] Issued Date : Expires :

Issued By :

☐ Individual ☐ Witness

Printed Name : Printed Name :

Address : Address :

Contact Info : Contact Info :

Signature : Signature :

Take Note

Notes

ENTRY # Month : M T W T F S S Page No.

Record Number : $Fee [ ] Thumb Print :

Notarized Type : Date Notarized :

Document Type : Document Date :

Service Performed

☐ Certification ☐ Acknowledgment ☐ Oath ☐ Jurat ☐

Identification

☐ Passport ☐ Known Personally ☐ ID Card ☐ Driver's License ☐

#ID Card

ID Number [ ] Issued Date : Expires :

Issued By :

☐ Individual ☐ Witness

Printed Name : Printed Name :

Address : Address :

Contact Info : Contact Info :

Signature : Signature :

Take Note

Notes

ENTRY # Month : M T W T F S S Page No.

Record Number : $Fee [ ] Thumb Print :

Notarized Type : Date Notarized :

Document Type : Document Date :

Service Performed

☐ Certification ☐ Acknowledgment ☐ Oath ☐ Jurat ☐

Identification

☐ Passport ☐ Known Personally ☐ ID Card ☐ Driver's License ☐

#ID Card

ID Number [ ] Issued Date : Expires :

Issued By :

☐ Individual ☐ Witness

Printed Name : Printed Name :

Address : Address :

Contact Info : Contact Info :

Signature : Signature :

Take Note

Notes

ENTRY # Month : M T W T F S S Page No.

Record Number : $Fee ☐ Thumb Print :

Notarized Type : Date Notarized :

Document Type : Document Date :

Service Performed

☐ Certification ☐ Acknowledgment ☐ Oath ☐ Jurat ☐

Identification

☐ Passport ☐ Known Personally ☐ ID Card ☐ Driver's License ☐

#ID Card

ID Number ☐ Issued Date : Expires :

Issued By :

☐ Individual ☐ Witness

Printed Name : Printed Name :

Address : Address :

Contact Info : Contact Info :

Signature : Signature :

Take Note

Notes

ENTRY # | Month : | M T W T F S S | Page No.

Record Number : $Fee Thumb Print :

Notarized Type : Date Notarized :

Document Type : Document Date :

Service Performed

☐ Certification ☐ Acknowledgment ☐ Oath ☐ Jurat ☐

Identification

☐ Passport ☐ Known Personally ☐ ID Card ☐ Driver's License ☐

#ID Card

ID Number Issued Date : Expires :

Issued By :

☐ Individual ☐ Witness

Printed Name : Printed Name :

Address : Address :

Contact Info : Contact Info :

Signature : Signature :

Take Note

Notes

ENTRY # Month : M T W T F S S Page No.

Record Number : $Fee [ ] Thumb Print :

Notarized Type : Date Notarized :

Document Type : Document Date :

Service Performed

☐ Certification ☐ Acknowledgment ☐ Oath ☐ Jurat ☐

Identification

☐ Passport ☐ Known Personally ☐ ID Card ☐ Driver's License ☐

#ID Card

ID Number [ ] Issued Date : Expires :

Issued By :

☐ Individual ☐ Witness

Printed Name : Printed Name :

Address : Address :

Contact Info : Contact Info :

Signature : Signature :

Take Note

Notes

ENTRY # Month : M T W T F S S Page No.

Record Number : $Fee [ ] Thumb Print :

Notarized Type : Date Notarized :

Document Type : Document Date :

Service Performed

☐ Certification ☐ Acknowledgment ☐ Oath ☐ Jurat ☐

Identification

☐ Passport ☐ Known Personally ☐ ID Card ☐ Driver's License ☐

#ID Card

ID Number [ ] Issued Date : Expires :

Issued By :

☐ Individual ☐ Witness

Printed Name : Printed Name :

Address : Address :

Contact Info : Contact Info :

Signature : Signature :

Take Note

Notes

ENTRY # Month : M T W T F S S Page No.

Record Number : $Fee [ ] Thumb Print :

Notarized Type : Date Notarized :

Document Type : Document Date :

Service Performed

☐ Certification ☐ Acknowledgment ☐ Oath ☐ Jurat ☐

Identification

☐ Passport ☐ Known Personally ☐ ID Card ☐ Driver's License ☐

#ID Card

ID Number [ ] Issued Date : Expires :

Issued By :

☐ Individual ☐ Witness

Printed Name : Printed Name :

Address : Address :

Contact Info : Contact Info :

Signature : Signature :

Take Note

Notes

ENTRY # Month : M T W T F S S Page No.

Record Number : $Fee ☐ Thumb Print :

Notarized Type : Date Notarized :

Document Type : Document Date :

Service Performed

☐ Certification ☐ Acknowledgment ☐ Oath ☐ Jurat ☐

Identification

☐ Passport ☐ Known Personally ☐ ID Card ☐ Driver's License ☐

#ID Card

ID Number ☐ Issued Date : Expires :

Issued By :

☐ Individual ☐ Witness

Printed Name : Printed Name :

Address : Address :

Contact Info : Contact Info :

Signature : Signature :

Take Note

Notes

ENTRY # Month : M T W T F S S Page No.

Record Number : $Fee [ ] Thumb Print :

Notarized Type : Date Notarized :

Document Type : Document Date :

Service Performed

☐ Certification ☐ Acknowledgment ☐ Oath ☐ Jurat ☐

Identification

☐ Passport ☐ Known Personally ☐ ID Card ☐ Driver's License ☐

#ID Card

ID Number [ ] Issued Date : Expires :

Issued By :

☐ Individual ☐ Witness

Printed Name : Printed Name :

Address : Address :

Contact Info : Contact Info :

Signature : Signature :

Take Note

Notes

ENTRY # Month : M T W T F S S Page No.

Record Number : $Fee [ ] Thumb Print :

Notarized Type : Date Notarized :

Document Type : Document Date :

Service Performed

☐ Certification ☐ Acknowledgment ☐ Oath ☐ Jurat ☐

Identification

☐ Passport ☐ Known Personally ☐ ID Card ☐ Driver's License ☐

#ID Card

ID Number [ ] Issued Date : Expires :

Issued By :

☐ Individual ☐ Witness

Individual	Witness
Printed Name :	Printed Name :
Address :	Address :
Contact Info :	Contact Info :
Signature :	Signature :

Take Note

Notes

ENTRY # Month : M T W T F S S Page No.

Record Number : $Fee ☐ Thumb Print :

Notarized Type : Date Notarized :

Document Type : Document Date :

Service Performed

☐ Certification ☐ Acknowledgment ☐ Oath ☐ Jurat ☐

Identification

☐ Passport ☐ Known Personally ☐ ID Card ☐ Driver's License ☐

#ID Card

ID Number ☐ Issued Date : Expires :

Issued By :

☐ Individual ☐ Witness

Printed Name : Printed Name :

Address : Address :

Contact Info : Contact Info :

Signature : Signature :

Take Note

Notes

ENTRY # Month : M T W T F S S Page No.

Record Number : $Fee Thumb Print :

Notarized Type : Date Notarized :

Document Type : Document Date :

Service Performed

☐ Certification ☐ Acknowledgment ☐ Oath ☐ Jurat ☐

Identification

☐ Passport ☐ Known Personally ☐ ID Card ☐ Driver's License ☐

#ID Card

ID Number Issued Date : Expires :

Issued By :

☐ Individual ☐ Witness

Printed Name : Printed Name :

Address : Address :

Contact Info : Contact Info :

Signature : Signature :

Take Note

Notes

ENTRY # Month : M T W T F S S Page No.

Record Number : $Fee Thumb Print :

Notarized Type : Date Notarized :

Document Type : Document Date :

Service Performed

☐ Certification ☐ Acknowledgment ☐ Oath ☐ Jurat ☐

Identification

☐ Passport ☐ Known Personally ☐ ID Card ☐ Driver's License ☐

#ID Card

ID Number Issued Date : Expires :

Issued By :

☐ Individual ☐ Witness

Printed Name : Printed Name :

Address : Address :

Contact Info : Contact Info :

Signature : Signature :

Take Note

Notes

ENTRY # Month : M T W T F S S Page No.

Record Number : $Fee ☐ Thumb Print :

Notarized Type : Date Notarized :

Document Type : Document Date :

Service Performed

☐ Certification ☐ Acknowledgment ☐ Oath ☐ Jurat ☐

Identification

☐ Passport ☐ Known Personally ☐ ID Card ☐ Driver's License ☐

#ID Card

ID Number ☐ Issued Date : Expires :

Issued By :

☐ Individual ☐ Witness

Printed Name : Printed Name :

Address : Address :

Contact Info : Contact Info :

Signature : Signature :

Take Note

Notes

ENTRY # Month : M T W T F S S Page No.

Record Number : $Fee [ ] Thumb Print :

Notarized Type : Date Notarized :

Document Type : Document Date :

Service Performed

☐ Certification ☐ Acknowledgment ☐ Oath ☐ Jurat ☐

Identification

☐ Passport ☐ Known Personally ☐ ID Card ☐ Driver's License ☐

#ID Card

ID Number [ ] Issued Date : Expires :

Issued By :

☐ Individual ☐ Witness

Printed Name : Printed Name :

Address : Address :

Contact Info : Contact Info :

Signature : Signature :

Take Note

Notes

ENTRY # Month : M T W T F S S Page No.

Record Number : $Fee [ ] Thumb Print :

Notarized Type : Date Notarized :

Document Type : Document Date :

Service Performed

☐ Certification ☐ Acknowledgment ☐ Oath ☐ Jurat ☐

Identification

☐ Passport ☐ Known Personally ☐ ID Card ☐ Driver's License ☐

#ID Card

ID Number [ ] Issued Date : Expires :

Issued By :

☐ Individual	☐ Witness
Printed Name :	Printed Name :
Address :	Address :
Contact Info :	Contact Info :
Signature :	Signature :

Take Note

Notes

ENTRY # Month : M T W T F S S Page No.

Record Number : $Fee ☐ Thumb Print :

Notarized Type : Date Notarized :

Document Type : Document Date :

Service Performed

☐ Certification ☐ Acknowledgment ☐ Oath ☐ Jurat ☐

Identification

☐ Passport ☐ Known Personally ☐ ID Card ☐ Driver's License ☐

#ID Card

ID Number ☐ Issued Date : Expires :

Issued By :

☐ Individual ☐ Witness

Printed Name : Printed Name :

Address : Address :

Contact Info : Contact Info :

Signature : Signature :

Take Note

Notes

ENTRY # Month : M T W T F S S Page No.

Record Number : $Fee [ ] Thumb Print :

Notarized Type : Date Notarized :

Document Type : Document Date :

Service Performed

☐ Certification ☐ Acknowledgment ☐ Oath ☐ Jurat ☐

Identification

☐ Passport ☐ Known Personally ☐ ID Card ☐ Driver's License ☐

#ID Card

ID Number [ ] Issued Date : Expires :

Issued By :

☐ Individual	☐ Witness
Printed Name :	Printed Name :
Address :	Address :
Contact Info :	Contact Info :
Signature :	Signature :

Take Note

Notes

ENTRY # Month : M T W T F S S Page No.

Record Number : $Fee Thumb Print :

Notarized Type : Date Notarized :

Document Type : Document Date :

Service Performed

☐ Certification ☐ Acknowledgment ☐ Oath ☐ Jurat ☐

Identification

☐ Passport ☐ Known Personally ☐ ID Card ☐ Driver's License ☐

#ID Card

ID Number Issued Date : Expires :

Issued By :

☐ Individual ☐ Witness

Individual	Witness
Printed Name :	Printed Name :
Address :	Address :
Contact Info :	Contact Info :
Signature :	Signature :

Take Note

Notes

ENTRY # Month : M T W T F S S Page No.

Record Number : $Fee Thumb Print :

Notarized Type : Date Notarized :

Document Type : Document Date :

Service Performed

☐ Certification ☐ Acknowledgment ☐ Oath ☐ Jurat ☐

Identification

☐ Passport ☐ Known Personally ☐ ID Card ☐ Driver's License ☐

#ID Card

ID Number Issued Date : Expires :

Issued By :

☐ Individual ☐ Witness

Printed Name : Printed Name :

Address : Address :

Contact Info : Contact Info :

Signature : Signature :

Take Note

Thank you !
We would really appreciate your
feedback, please send us a email to:
ritirra@gmail.com

www.ingramcontent.com/pod-product-compliance
Lightning Source LLC
LaVergne TN
LVHW070855210926
848482LV00016B/943